# ANIMAL WALK

# Animal Walk

John O'Neill

Turnstone Press

Turnstone Press gratefully acknowledges the assistance of the Canada Council and the Manitoba Arts Council.

Turnstone Press
607-100 Arthur Street
Winnipeg, Manitoba
Canada R3B 1H3

This book was printed by Hignell Printing Limited for Turnstone Press.

Printed in Canada

Cover illustration: Nicole de Montbrun

Cover design: Robert MacDonald, MediaClones

Canadian Cataloguing in Publication Data

O'Neill, John, 1959-

Animal walk

Poems.
ISBN 0-88801-129-6

I. Title.

PS8579.N44A73 1988 C811'.54 C88-098108-3
PR9199.3.O53A73 1988

For A. Labriola

Some of these poems have appeared in

*Event, The Fiddlehead, The Malahat Review,*
*Queen's Quarterly, Rubicon,*
*University College Review.*

Thanks to

Tony Labriola, George McWhirter,
Janet Loretta, Linda Copman-Sebesta,
Jacob Zilber, Dennis Cooley

## CONTENTS

### BORDERS

## DEER DANCING BEFORE A MIRROR

## ANIMAL WALK

# 1.
# BORDERS

A night, ten villages, a mountain,
A black, gold-studded Leviathan.

— G.E. Clancier

## THE RIVER'S WINDOW

Sundays,
her father
carried her on
his shoulders, a bundle through
the maze of filthy cages to the zoo's
aquarium. Where, under
blue-green shade,
between whispers, they
unfolded, together,
and watched the
porpoises and whales. Sometimes
a small beluga would
apply his brakes
and beat like a fretting heart against the
squeak of glass. Now,

years gone, most without a trace,
her father's held to a crippled chair.
She follows a path through the trees
down to where the St. Lawrence
arches its wing. She studies the waves
prays for fluke or fin, the moment
to take back with her, a long
perfect feather to her father in their
shrinking apartment. And she doesn't lie
when the river's window
surrenders nothing
but its chopped reflection of the
late afternoon.

## YELLOW HOUSE, CAPE BRETON

Yellow house, curve
in the road, slit
fish eye through
a lid of fog.
The sea laps
its inside walls,
curtains float with
ribbons of kelp.
Imagine
a family in a skiff
sculling
from room to room,
their spiked siamese
paddling a mahogany chest.
The front door opens,
possessions leak,
water meets water.
A yellow house
dissolves its holdings,
blurs with memory
in the proximate
rooms of the sea.

## BITTER

Summer around here
is a milkweed cracked open,
some green stuff, but mostly white
leaking out into
miles and miles of blank sky.
You carry the flowers of bitterroot
from a field of horses.
Horses are dumber than
a bag of hammers, you say.
And, with your own long face
more severe than any black beauty,
you stoop by a fence.
Tie the stems into a chain,
your fingers fretting
over their own hard elegance.
Twenty times longer
than the last one,
it's a river of snares
for anything lost in Durham County.
You lie down in the long grass
your shoulders cranked back.
The weed stains your nervous hands.
You can't steal farm land,
but I think of you as a thief
ripping off the sky,
the shameless and
wrecked ribbons of bitterroot.

## THE WISHING CHAIR

From a band of gypsies
she bought the chair—
then, hypnotized by what she wanted
most from her last years
she rocked, teetered on
the edge of dream.
But only clouds gathered
or a speckled mouse went a-
cross the floor
or, once, an owl,
white as milk,
floundered through
and mopped dust from her diningroom table.
But this was not what
she'd wished for, sitting
in the wishing chair.

She died there, turned almost to oak.
Her only son found her after
three years he'd been gone, never
having written. But he entered her cabin
as if it were a church, open to
his sudden conversion.

## GRANDMOTHER

Birdhead. This is what it
comes to, your stringy body
flaked as an eggshell,
browns like sparrows' wings,
fretting over your dinner plate.
Larger wings
beat at your death's door.

Outside, in the smoked window,
a snowy owl. He's old, whiskered,
but the world still pivots
on his shoulders.

What turns your head?
Already laid out, draining breath,
but for a slight, wintergreen
breeze rippling your nightgown.
We feed you words through a dropper—
quality, sanctity. A slit wing,
or quaking ball of tissue,
you are unborn to us again.

## NEARLY BORN

Amniotic light, filtered through
skin and stars. The beginning is
slow, the sky revving up, heating
up. By the chopped ocean, you
hug yourself as though the rising wind
might take bits of you.
But it wants everything.
At your feet the limestone shatters,
earth and sky near convergence.
You are the flooding eye
as the storm breaks.

Something spins towards birth.
Lightning
splits the sky but only
rain drops. Wind
tries to suck you up a
descending funnel but you
plant yourself in stunted spruce,
gripped in the earth's stirrups.
You are behind yourself, inside
yourself, thinking about houses,
family, doors. Wanting out
(your grip tightens)
and the whole of nature falling, pounding
double fists on your head.

The clouds go, disperse like mist,
and you watch the shadow of your fear
sweep the sunlight back. Your head
is clear, back to calm, vision
without darkness. Nothing
nearly born.

## OCEAN AND ISLANDS

We paddle between islands
and watch the strong gulls
circle our canoe
though the sun is the sky's centre.
Its waves of light are blurred wheel spokes
birds, drifting, can pass through,
or they dive like bombers after fish
that contain in their probing knife heads
long empty corridors,
museum rooms to be filled by evolution.
Sometimes the ocean current is too strong.
It makes a joke of our work
as if an electrical wire's been
pulled from our muscles.
Gull-waste
left to our own strength.

## BLACK TUSK

Not all is work, muscles'
complaints, or insects'
needles drawn through
your skin. There is
(for instance)
the glacial air
kissing your mouth, or
the hoary marmot
carrying his lunchbag
body across a slice of snow. And pausing
to watch you
gather around
the cairn of your breathing.

Not all fear—look
straight up the rock
chimney, negotiate
in your mind its
flaked ladder. Or
crouch in the peaked
shade, see the clouds
unpeel below,
leaving the meadows
ripening green.

Best of all, descend.
Skate through
halls of trees
or on the firm
toboggan of your back. Soaked from
hair to socks
but already
remembering

the mountain's
active
reverence.

## STORM WARNING

Slit-eyed
clouds roll
across the glacier.
On the ice spin
corkscrews of wind,
boring the
perpetual
ache of its tongue.
The scree and this
staircase of rock
appear to shift—
barometers drop
easy as dominoes
all along the coast.

We sober ourselves,
bolt windows,
secure the latches
of our coats, Gore-
tex and down.
Caulk the seams
with assurances. But
we've no chance
of safe descent—
lightning
stirring the swill
of memory behind us.

## SNAPSHOT

From Canada's thin end
she sends a picture of herself;
near naked, but with a dark shawl
pushing up her shoulders. Looking,
you don't care where you live, how far,
you want to eat through.

What can you send in return?
Not one of yourself, bare on bearskin,
preening on the coast, or
with eyes hawked, hooded, leading
man with muscles pencilled in.
Rather, hold your breath, snap your
heart in its flight; a scarf of shadow
soothes your trembling throat.

## SMALL TREE

You are not a body of light, that's a game
the awaking sun plays, its farther reaches
spilling onto your body, sudden, and just as
suddenly gone with your plunge into darkness,
the lake's portion of night. Out, weightless
on your back, waterbug-hovering, waterwings
spreading you forward, then, again, the black
lake, you heading back to shore, one foot
subversive just below the surface

and up over rocks, sand, quick bowls of water
where your heels press in, reminding me
your body is heavy, unruly, unable
between boulders (mountain scat)
to explore the forest's high reaches,
like a sparrow, or even a fat bird to press
upward with a conjuring of feathers.
You're here to stay,
except for brief, dreamy forays,
between where the lake sweeps
and the mountains halt,
an animal dreamt by the world,
accepting the rock and the water as
a small tree does.

## FAT WOMAN IN WAPITI CAMPGROUND

She's
beautiful as a tree.
Though she lumbers through
stands of fir on her way to
the pit toilet. You can
tell by her eyes,
or her big voice that
shakes out, clean laundry in it.
She smiles at us, says
"Gosh, it's nice, isn't it," sweeps
an arm across
dog-eared mountains, as if she's
pulled them from the hat of her hand.
She doffs the light,
steps into the wooden room,
and I imagine her there
wielding a pen-knife, or larger blade,
carving on the small interior,
the way she must carve
dreams on the inside of herself,
across the breathing walls;
or, pour them like milk
from her heart's concentric rings.

# ICEFIELDS PARKWAY

Gas-station attendant,
up to *here* with tourists.
His stained overalls hang
from goosebumps the size of quarters.
He wields the steel muzzle,
fixes it to the lip of the tank.
The ticking pump starts.
For a moment I imagine
the tube connects
intestinally
to the surrounding mountains,
that they'll slowly deflate,
solemnly fart the stuff
that keeps us going. We pay
through the rolled window,
the attendant's
hoop of black hands
snaps out bills, coupons, oil-stink
threading the car.
Engine begun, he
sprints back through the streaked light,
foots open the door,
warms hands over
a coffee. His smaller
goosebumps shrink.

## PIGEON-TOED

Saskatchewan. I'm walking
beside railway tracks towards cloud.
My shadow's pulled far by the horizon,
the way everything here
wants to lie down. The train is stopped
a half-mile back. It throws a dinosaur
shadow across the dug soil,
the flat land. I can see a bonfire
in a cornfield—like open-heart surgery.

The local bar is full of locals.
They're kicking and shaking on the floor,
they have this epilepsy that comes
from being able to see too far.
A tumbled drunk stares at my shoes,
but his eyes are crossed, like everybody's—
the train tracks, if you follow them all the way,
start to run pigeon-toed.

## ACCIDENT, ALGONQUIN PARK

Highway 60,
blind with rain, we
barely make the corner.
Then, hardening into focus,
a truck
on its side by the road.
Pull over.
A police car nearby,
but not a soul.

I imagine the trucker,
his grin a slash,
slogging through swamps,
expelled from his accident.
The officer
tracks him through
movie rain—
himself dreaming
of some Yukon tale, the Northwest Mounted
hacking through bush to cuff
a fur-capped killer. I play
the film out
in my mind.

But this is Algonquin. No murder.
A sleepy driver
and a deer springing
sudden from a box of trees;
and the trucker,
semi-conscious,
fastened to a new set of
relations.

Us, also. The park
goes friendly, its
expanse manageable. We drive
carefully from that broken needle.
The haystack wilderness
shrinks around us.

## SPRUCE BOG BOARDWALK

The boardwalk
twists through swamps. Trees like
antlers
knock together, bode
eclipse. On my left,
a kettle bog, mineral
bath for the unwary walker,
overgrown
with moss and tea.
Fallen through,
the body is preserved,
though the skin goes black,
leathery as a football. Thinking of it,
my thoughts turn muddy,
dark and malicious. Picture some
black-robe
crawling with relics,
plunging through muck,
himself made relic,
argillite shrine.
I feel the urge to follow
as one feels
the tug of a waterfall, or
coax of a deadly height.
But my head clears in time.
Still, I've been made grey.
The boardwalk grid
keeps out the bog,
preserves me from
further preservation.

## HOUSE AND ROAD

There are voices on this side of the road.
Voices, stirred by wind, perhaps
soaked into leaves.
They rise up from their catacombs.

This place,
patch on a larger world,
blurred picture from a bus window.
Passing, how many
looked upon this road, this house,
not knowing
we curled up with roots,
fingers in the thick dark soil.
The living once moved
among its hollows, vigorous
over stacks of wood.

A child I once knew saw the possibilities.
Perhaps not, eyes were small, hard
to fully open. But felt in
the dizziness of the heart, a chrysalis
cracking, a dark figure, there.
Ghosts from the road
told incantations, that all the fears, desires
would find sanctuary.
This was deception.
An autumn world
jests with the heart,
the insistent
flaw in a child.

## STILL LIFE, TAYLOR RIVER

We stop by the stream, the water
tossing up whiteness. In fall,
salmon spawn. Now, only we two
returning from a grey, drizzly
weekend at Long Beach. Your
photographer's eye
pulls you from the car.

Perched near the umbrella of water,
I dream of home. You, of the picture.
In your mind the trees go negative,
the world has borders that start
just beyond my head.

The photo doesn't turn out. You blame
the developing. I recall nothing
of the camera's clipped load and fire,
not if the cap had been unscrewed or
the lens smeared with spray. Now,
without the picture, its stark containment,
the trees and river and rocks blur
irredeemably with all of your
unkept exteriors, your on-the-ways.

## MADAWASKA RIVER

I

We lower the canoe
through white-caps of air.
Soon, its crescent moon
clips through the foam, wind
and detergent making
a beerhead on Loonskin Lake.
Life-jackets
don't preserve us from
thoughts of disaster, the way
a storm can
scare up
on hind legs,
a black bear from thorny sleep.
Minutes, and we're
piling up waves in the lake's centre.

Work. Nothing less.
Paddles
fringe with water.
Muscles un-
thread, needles of sweat.
Ahead,
a ribbon marks the spot,
shorn patch of earth where
we will unfurl the flag of our tent,
collect ourselves on land. Later,
oily sleep.

## II

As if we haven't slept, or dreamt, gliding
above the river in a canoe of memory—we've
been here before.
A moose's head,
big as a drum,
pushes through pines,
wonders just what we're up to.
*Gareem*? goes the gruff inquiry,
the thick foreign tongue.

Even the loon's
long rope of song
is beyond us.

III

We cut a swathe through lakes:
Loonskin, Lost, Hare and
Buck. We're fastened
to our map, though it's
wet as a kleenex,
the pins
floating on
twin points of light.

We search for the centre.

Not the river.
Not this time,
but for something essential,
prize to be uncovered,
an artifact,
or, better,
a moose's antlers,
inset with shells, tiled like
a polished skull. Something we can
carry back with us and say
Yes, this is it, this is what we found,
always find there,
real, like bone, but
jewelled, stuck with its own
bright history.
We want it both ways:
how the finder
creates, is created by,
what he finds.

## IV

Our canoe
lifts from the water. We've
discovered, repaired
nothing. The lake's skin,
from our incision,
every second
stitches, darkly
heals.

# 2.
# DEER DANCING BEFORE A MIRROR

I watched the bear too long—until my face became that of a bear watching a man.

— J. Michael Yates,
*The Great Bear Lake Meditations*

## FLASHER

Black. Rain
punches the tent.
Rivulets

rib under the groundsheet.
Now
and often

a stroke of thunder

or lightning
when
the tuxedoed
sky unzippers.

## THE LOST JOCKEY

On the last track, his
home stretch, neck
on neck with
*Jacob's Pleasure*,
he finds himself,
both he and his mount,
hurtling through
lodgepole pines
across a furlong
of flowers. The horse
doesn't blink,
still squirts steam,
and hooves compress
like hot irons
the leafy pad.
The jockey is disturbed,
a chill rubs his spine,
but he fastens again
to the thoroughbred,
assimilates
their lostness
in the drive of
a mutual animal.
The crowd's gone,
the competing riders,
and the finish line's
an indefinite reprieve.
Horse and rider
bite deeply
into one another,
for the moment
mated to one direction.

## A BARN BURNS DOWN

in the middle of somewhere,
north
Saskatchewan winter.
Flames
flap skyward
and a single horse
bolts from the room
sparks
streaming from its teeth.
Neighbours, helpless,
huddle together,
monked in blankets,
and a small boy
jokes about
roasting wienies—
his mother
smacks him so hard that
for a moment
the fire's forgotten.
But,
driving off,
you keep seeing that
spooked beast,
its ribs' bellows,
and all the farmers' eyes
going
up, around, up, a-
round, the flared
nostrils, dark.

## SPORTS

Fly-fisher,
knee-deep,
but deeper in
the throat of his boots.
He casts his thoughts
and they idle on the surface.
He isn't thinking
of the smaller life, clam
castanets, pin-eyes or claws that
quake in the riverbed, or of
the thin snake that, for an instant,
makes a lace on his rubbers.
He dreams of the yanking out,
the reel humming, and the hooked
fish in air, its clock
unplugged. In a month
this river will flame salmon,
other sportsmen will
wade through with sleepy nets.
But do not think this man is different,
stoic in the cold stream, picking
the river's teeth. His brain
drifts. Pray that
a whale or shark might mistake
and swallow it whole, and him
strung on his line. Only then will he
eat fish.

## HUNTER AND CARIBOU

Their hieroglyphs
Trail in the snow, unspool
In the hunter's arena.
Sights caught up
In the dark toss of antlers
He warms, then
Eats his gun.

In army fatigues
He steps to the circle
The cooling zone
Of the animal's
Spent proximity. Then
Trains its skull
On an underworld.

## SLEEPLESS

Across your night
moose and bear
leave their spoor. You feel
antlers descend, dull
throb between your
shoulder-blades. Your life is
a small creature, barely
perceived. But in this dream
migration begins:
geese and caribou
pull shadows across
imagined walls. Everything is
crazed into conspiracy:
your bed rocking on
a pillar of bog. You watch yourself
watching them. A cow
stares back. But nothing
rises to its face,
your brain swimming like an otter,
dreaming of largeness,
the weather tumbling down.
Inside her, you turn.
You sleep in that familiar,
inaccessible place. Trees, starfire,
a platoon of faceless animals
marches blind above a plain.
The night wind unhooks
curtains of leaves. Waking, you're even
farther away. Your tent spills open
with sleepless sun. The animals
drop you out again.

## CONFUSION OF TONGUES

In my dream, across
a red brook, at
the end of the spoor,
three laughing
pre-Raphaelite girls
knead and shampoo
a grizzly. Wolves
tug at their skirts.
The girls
speak a language
I don't know.
When I cross
the water and talk,
the animals
bolt for cover
and the girls
launch sticks and stones
and pursue me through
a gabbling stream.
Then, at the chase's
crux, on a plank of
rock, my back
forced to a wall of air,
I snap awake
and find myself
in that animal mood.
Sweaty, exhausting,
I hear my own
malformed words,
tongue
muscle-bound,
not like those
slender hands
kneading
the dank animal.

## HER FEAR IS WHALE

Her fear is whale.
Her fearful rise from a
rippling bed is
an unveiling before whale,
her trembling,
venerable skin. Even
in the warm-mouthed morning,
the anxiety that is whale
anchors its freezing
eye in her heart,
claiming everything,
splinters of her hope
collecting there,
heaped like iron filings. Splinters
of what she dreams
(how she might swim free)
stuck in the whale's
dive and sounding
at the bottom of her dark bay.
Unfathomably. Her life
surrounded by lobster-traps,
and fishermen in rain gear
trolling torn nets through water that's
rapt as a mirror.

## THE MOOSE IS THERE

She doesn't see
the shadow of the moose
reflecting in the lake.
Not even something
in the corner of her eye
like the memory
of a dream that
in the acid light
quickly dissolves.
The moose is there
steering fork-lift antlers,
huge and shagged as a squall-line
then, gracelessly,
steps through a hole.
Then, she looks, and the lake is
still. No shadow (that is, no
reflection of the tree where
the moose's shadow crossed)
disturbs its surface.

She becomes withdrawn.
Recedes deeper,
deeper into herself
until, soon, mirrors
she looks in
dissolve in light.
Not even
a thicket of memories
tears at her clothes.
Her shadow—nil.
The wilderness keeps her out,
and she, diving,
over the clear lake
of this restriction,
dissolves.

## WISEMAN

Fire
and the rawness of the wound
but when it was done
a frost came.
Her husband
blew into his hands
and rubbed her a flame.

The three guests stood near the animals.
Dumb-struck,
wearing animal masks,
their hearts wagging.

But these were men of ceremony.
They dropped their donkey looks,
unpacked gifts and words,
and cut the ribbon to
begin things.

One dreamed an angel on a fig tree.
Another, childless, blessed the day
as the birth of all childhood.
The third, younger, worried.
He said nothing
but kept an eye
on the red straw place,
the infant with the onyx eyes
between scraping hooves.

## TOGETHER, MOVING THROUGH

I can feel my mind growing.
Or, at least, shifting its feet,
sparring in a ring of light.
The sun came over the ridge
with brilliance and arrows
and I'm pinned by its shafts
in the blood meadow. The cut
mountain face, the tiny
fists of flowers, these
force me to a question. The forever
river, snake between ranges,
is a fire in my throat. But an ease
eases my stride for how we two,
together, with packs and field glasses,
walk between prodding trees
and need not speak. We need
not speak.

## VOICES

The wilderness wants everything.
It speaks its peace clearly,
the fir trees sing,
the ice depresses a string.
But, though I've
not listened (zeroed in, absorbed
by the thrumming of my blood)
the wilderness sends
a small whirring bug
like a pill to dissolve in my throat.

# 3.
# ANIMAL WALK

All animals are holy,
They are themselves.

—Ralph Gustafson,
*In the Everglades*

I am a brother of jackels,
and a companion of ostriches.
My skin turns black and falls from
me,
and my bones burn with heat.
My lyre is turned to mourning,
and my pipe to the voice of those
who weep.

— Job 30:29-31

## THEOLOGY AT ROBSON BITE

Job's God
made the leviathan
who swallows us all.
His mouth is wide,
a horizon. Faces
blanch, ferried
on his tongue. Disaster
always remembers
the pious (Job's
eggshell fists
cracked by a bolt).

And what of the small
orca out by the dock
sunning in piebald
near the amused fisherman—
will he sense the shape
or moment of the harpoon's
fire,
and the fisherman who everyday
rides on the broad back of
death as if it were the sea?

## RACCOONS

A claw on the air, then
creaking, like a barndance.
The raccoons move in. Over-
head, they unpack their
bags. Their eyes saucer
when we open the door.

What to do? There are always
men to call. They
wreck property, smuggle
disease. Why couldn't
they be smaller, negligible,
like mice, death
swept out with the dust.

At night, the house lives. We
ache, for they are settling in.
We wish
our dog would take care of it.

## A RABBIT

struck carrying its furred parcel
across the blinkered road.
I slip my hands under
lift the body from its oily scab,
wrap it in my shirt.
I drive the accident to my house,
keep the rabbit bundled,
its eyes still wet, body warm,
wait for the shock to subside,
its nightmare of a heavy, chromed bird
slicing air a foot above the criss-
crossed ground. Thump and squeal.
My little brother won't look.
For him death is contagious
as if the stopped
business of rabbit
will infect him, start him
chewing his own thinness
deliberately away.

## THE BEAVER

His pelt was our first currency.
Still
one needn't think of this,
watching, for pleasure,
his dark body,
a coat hung from the spike of his teeth.
Those four incisors
would grow into a cage
if he didn't chaw the earth.
He doesn't taste leisure,
his isn't the sedentary life,
and his dam keeps him
from the naturalists and children
who, active, lounge on the shore.
But everytime he falls
from the nibbling hot air
into the stream
he takes a twig
from the long house of his labours.
The cold bite of water
has pleasure in it.

## BRAIN FOOD

The fish rub together
In their kingdom of crossed swords.

Like gangs of samurai
Armoured in links of silver.

We are watchmen
Evolution's brainy caste

Adapting their features (fish-
Lungs, flippers)
In the duty of our leisure.

To net them for dinner.

## ELEPHANT

My mind is empty.
My mind is pale and empty.

An elephant stands with his eye at the keyhole.

## HUNTING FLESH

The details accumulate
—hooves, knees, dewlap,
neck, antlers with
a thin film on their cross.
The ingredients shift, and your finger
coils on the trigger.
But in the tightening,
the breath's delay,
the moose is already
roll-calling his body
across the meadow
behind a boneyard of trees.
Every animal
you've yet to stalk
is cradled in that deer's rack,
full caribou herds
migrate through
the cirque of his spine.
A ghost of strong flesh,
black, urine-smelly,
steps between you and that
year of dinners:
your body's empathy.
You can't shoot
and the loss is a delicacy.

## ARCTIC SPRING

Narwhal
outfitted like
traditional
Inuit, spears and
talons, the whole
arctic their
hunting grounds.
Northern
lights fasten above,
jewelled
asps on the breastplates of a
black
starless army.
Smearing
ice with
caribou blood, morning
crosses the air.
And listen:
a high-pitched
wail
as if
something got
caught in
the lifting drape of dark.
See its
hoofprints in the snow,
and fear when
the spring waters
break, pressing
the moon, a
whistling
lung, up against
a stiff
curtain of cloud.

## WOLF CALL, HARE LAKE

More than wolf
frozen before us, knees
locked, lips curled.
More than a wolf's
sleek head,
throat rippling,
bending one sound. The air,
a moebius strip,
a spiral. The ear
folding
in on
itself, a wolf
call. Eyes set
headlights on either side of that howl,
echoing,
returning to the hill,
more than a hawk
answering a gloved hand.
Not a thing in itself, of itself.
But binding things together,
constricting breath,
wolf call,
jagged and hidden,
all the teeth in the broken jaw
of this howling winter night.

## BEAR

Having scrubbed hands
and face, scrubbed and
flossed teeth of four
days camping, accumulated
camp-fire funk, I step
out from the bright toilet
and meet a bear. I can only
see his eyes, fiery points,
so the whole darkness behind
might be his body. Can't
rinse him away, he just swings his head
and I hear his low sound like
an idling car. Step backward,
into the bathroom's glow
and something in that bear brain snaps,
he follows his fire-cracker eyes
back into the sticky woods. I return
to the bathroom, watch my face's
white sink refill, and reflect on
just what it was the bear saw, or didn't see,
what my full eyes, in the light, resembled,
what quality of darkness lay behind.

## BELUGA WHALE BIRTH

She gives birth
(takes nothing)
squeezes his
Casper ghost
out like toothpaste.
The baby
circles the
strange dirigible
probes
for the way back in.
But scolded by
her revolving eye
and with a
swat to his bare
whale bum
he enters his hunger
starts his
spiral life.

His brooding mother
(though white as blizzards)
seeks
to eat her own tail
to come full circle
in that wound of sea
while
her little one
turns near the bottom,
by the
ocean's plug.
Her large
shapeless death
is drained out in advance
through his
heart's baleen.

## THE MOOSE

is unanswerable,
his strangeness made relic,
antlers like carved wings,
silence filling his snout to
burst. Large and too much animal.
Moving through twilit bush, the ticking
wilderness is stopped by his alarm,
coming upon you by the lake, his
final body propped up like an ark
on inadequate legs. Approach his giant
hesitation, lay the gift of your
stare at his hooves: nothing is revealed.
Grind his antlers down, taste his
*pharmacon*, or wrap yourself in
the wind of his hide. And enter
your gods wearing his armour
of silence, monstrosity.

## GOAT

sure-footed,
horned mountaineer,
Moses with his weathered reason
packing tablets under a blanket.
You circle the horns of the earth,
fugitive of the nether regions,
icicle spiked and your
hooves leaving teethmarks
in the high terrain.
Your fur a lying cloud.
Your fur a waterfall
taller than light
with whorls of river rapids.
I suspect
when Noah launched his crib,
you and your kind
waited on a peak of air
or stood on the moon until
the earth inhaled.
You're in my brain,
you perch atop fissures
with horns as comforting
as a spear gripped in hand
and your trail leaves signs,
hieroglyphs, diadems,
a braille for the unbelievers.

## BEHEMOTH

the unspeakable,
shape-shifting monster,
mount of the accuser,
holds the warm sceptre
bone in his jaws.
Given dominion
over all the earth's creatures,
Genesis inverted,
the impenetrable
tortoise-shell Bible.
God grips the dice,
cracks his fist to unleash
*ichthys*,
snake-eyed,
the dark bestiary.

Bow down before the mute king,
creature of the sea
creature of the land
on his skull
the relic cross, antlered.
Knock at the door of his ribs
so you might enter.
Drink from his hooves' cup
so you might marry
the bridegroom,
in a suit of gills
Jesus the coelacanth.
And do not question
this leash upon your heart,
or your gored reason,
the horned eschatology.

## THE ANIMALS THINK

(I am) going to venture through
going to live according to
and drop
fur fang and
into the clear cold
animals think
is not what the animals think
this is what the animals
the darkness is a river as long as
as dark as
the dark
listen
they say
with their flickering tongues
shout
with the long loop of their howl
dark river hill
this is what the
animal
the darkness is a whale (river hill) as long as
deep as dark
the animals think
surrender
get rough
venture through
live according to
drop
dark river as dark as wet as
drop your face into it
shatter on the river
do not speak
do not say
drop drop self surface again
think animals think
and not what the animals think

## DEER DANCING BEFORE A MIRROR

A mirror
in the middle of the trees
like a doll
or bottle found
in the rift of a mountain.
Deer gather to drink
but find they
tap a hard tile
or slide under their legs.

They move in slow motion,
dreaming of themselves.
Their trance is doubled
and no wave
or thrashing fish
can snap their attention
back to deer business.

## ANIMALS

live above
judgement
in their
state of grace.
Grizzlies, shagged
goats, no
baroque seraphim, no
visible wings—
but the comfortable
necessity, the raw
need, a balancing
scheme of things.

Bear stories
are often of
hellish descents.
But a bear
goes unblamed,
really, like
a cyclone of fur,
or nameless
tsunami drowned
in its own path. Pitiable

murder-suicide.
                                        We,
though, name names
(only human)
and murder ourselves
in the animal's pelt,
wearing
necessity's skin.
The animals
in their Edens
sniff for the boundaries
of our
benevolence.